Original title:
Seeds of Serenity

Copyright © 2025 Creative Arts Management OÜ
All rights reserved.

Author: Wyatt Kensington
ISBN HARDBACK: 978-1-80567-009-4
ISBN PAPERBACK: 978-1-80567-089-6

Misty Days of Reflection

In a foggy coat, I wander wide,
My thoughts play peek-a-boo, they hide.
With pancakes flipping and birds in flight,
I sip my tea and laugh at light.

The Art of Resting in Nature

I found a spot, the sun's warm hug,
Laid in the grass, on a friendly rug.
A squirrel passed by, gave me a wink,
He looked at me like, 'Time to rethink!'

Illuminated Paths of Peace

Bumblebees buzzing, they dance with flair,
They twirl and spin without a care.
Sunbeams giggle on the ground,
While my lost socks finally are found!

The Stillness Between Heartbeats

In the quiet, a laugh erupts,
A bouquet of thoughts, all kinds of ups.
The breeze whispers jokes, oh so free,
Nature's comedy club, just for me!

Subtle Shifts of the Heart

My heart once danced like a flea,
But tripped on thoughts of brie.
It swayed to jazz, then skipped a beat,
Only to land on something sweet.

With every grin, it jumps about,
Like a puppy pulling me out.
It giggles at my winter socks,
And throws confetti at the clocks.

The Breath of Serene Spaces

In a field of lazy wit,
Clouds wear hats, just to fit.
The daisies chat with passing bees,
While trees play hide and seek with leaves.

A breeze whispers silly plans,
As ants march on with tiny cans.
Squirrels giggle in their nests,
And even the rabbits take breaks for rests.

Resilience in Flourishing Green

A cactus wore a flower crown,
While ferns complained of being brown.
The grass held tight to every joke,
As butterflies learned to poke and poke.

A weed claimed it was the star,
Announcing dreams of going far.
Together they formed quite a scene,
In this quirky patch of vibrant green.

Embraced by Golden Silence

The sun closed its eyes for a nap,
While shadows began a playful slap.
A turtle chuckled, slow and wise,
As birds raced past in a blur of skies.

In silence, laughter found its home,
As crickets struck up the evening's poem.
Beneath the stars, the night joined in,
And even the moon wore a goofy grin.

Whispers of the Quiet Mind

In the garden of thoughts, squirrels play,
Finding acorns to brighten their day.
Mice wear tiny hats, sipping tea,
Crafting plans for a grand jubilee.

The breeze tells jokes, leaves start to giggle,
While worms dance in tune, a wiggle and wiggle.
Clouds in the sky join the fun parade,
As bunnies hop round, in a playful charade.

Germination of Tranquility

A flower sprouted in my sock drawer,
Shouting, 'Hey buddy, can't take this bore!'
Bees dressed in tuxedos buzz around,
As laughter erupts from the soft ground.

The petals complain, they need a vacation,
Wishing for beaches and sun for reflection.
But instead, they giggle at raindrop's tease,
"Is it a shower? Or just a sneeze?"

The Calm Within the Chaos

In the storm of socks, one brave shoe sings,
Waltzing through storms, it twirls on springs.
A fish in a puddle dons a fine tie,
"Welcome to chaos, let's give it a try!"

The umbrella, confused, tries to take flight,
While ants play chess in the flickering light.
A cat walks by, with a crown on its head,
Declaring, "I rule, now everyone spread!"

Nature's Gentle Embrace

A tree told a secret to the windy sky,
"Why do you whistle? Please tell me, oh my!"
The leaves chuckled softly at such a plight,
Each branch swayed gently, a delightful sight.

The rocks discussed wisdom beneath the moon,
"How long must we sit? It's getting monsoon!"
But a butterfly flew with a giggle and sway,
"Let's dance in the raindrops, come join the ballet!"

Sowing Solitude's Gift

In a garden where giggles sprout,
Funny thoughts dance all about.
Planting jokes like daisies bright,
Sunshine blooms in sheer delight.

Raindrops giggle from the sky,
Tickling flowers, oh my, oh my!
Worms wear glasses, they're quite keen,
Teaching bees how to be seen.

Composting laughs, the soil's rich,
Every chuckle finds a niche.
Visitors arrive with silly hats,
Teacups filled with chatting cats.

Tending plants that like to tease,
Branches swaying in the breeze.
This patch grows more than blooms or greens,
With laughter stitched in all the seams.

The Garden of Gentle Thoughts

In the garden of easy cheer,
Funny ideas sprout right here.
Butterflies hold a comedy night,
With twinkling stars as their spotlight.

Roses share their silliest tales,
While daisies giggle in their gales.
Every petal wears a grin,
As the fun begins to spin.

The sun winks down through leaves of jade,
Every shadow throws a shade.
Laughter echoes in the air,
Even trees join in the affair.

Bumblebees buzzing jokes aloud,
As crickets chirp, attracting crowd.
In this plot, joy takes the lead,
A harvest full of laughter's seed.

Nurtured by the Silence

In the stillness, whispers play,
Silly giggles chase the gray.
Roots of humor stretch so wide,
Tickling toes on nature's ride.

In silence, the crickets plot,
Funny pranks that they have sought.
Breeze delivers each light jest,
Making even the stones feel blessed.

Sunbeams shoot like playful darts,
Cheering up the heart of hearts.
Flowers wear their best disguise,
Turnip tops with charming ties.

With a sarcasm-filled refrain,
Joy blossoms even through the rain.
No storm can steal this cheerful sight,
Where giggles bloom with pure delight.

Echoes of Tranquil Waters

By the brook where laughter flows,
Silly faces on the crows.
Ripples carry jokes and glee,
Making fish find harmony.

Pebbles giggle as they skip,
Water sings a jovial trip.
Frogs in ties do comedy,
Creating quite a sight to see.

The ducks quack out a punchline,
Tickled waves dance and align.
With every splash, a chuckle flies,
Even the lilies can't disguise.

In the calm, where echoes play,
Silly thoughts come out to play.
Nature's humor, vast and grand,
Weaving joy throughout the land.

The Silent Bloom of Hope

In a garden so quiet, plants hold a chat,
Feigning to grow while debating the cat.
Petunias in pajamas, giggling with glee,
Who knew that daisies loved tea parties free?

Under moonlight, they sway, sharing jokes,
About how the carrots wear fashionable cloaks.
While birds chirp the songs of their leafy delight,
The flowers just chuckle, 'Oh what a night!'

Whispering Grasslands

In the tall grass, the jokes spread like fire,
Each blade winks at rabbits, their laughter gets higher.
A squirrel with a hat, oh what a sight!
Steals acorns from pigeons, then takes to flight.

Cows in the field hold conferences vast,
Debating on who is the best chef at last.
While frogs in the pond croak witty retorts,
Every leap seems to pair with comical shorts.

Natural Farewell to Worry

The trees hold a summit, their leaves all a-flutter,
With whispers of troubles, the woodpecker's utter.
A hedgehog stands up with a sarcastic grin,
'You worry too much, just let the fun in!'

Wildflowers chuckle at clouds passing by,
'Do they ever trample? Oh, what a sigh!'
Yet birds chirp tunes that evict all the dread,
As the sun sets down, painting golds overhead.

The Harmony of Hidden Roots

Beneath the soil, where the whispers abide,
The roots share gossip, oh what a ride!
With jesters of fungi and jesting old stones,
They laugh at the breezes that tickle their bones.

While branches above let out giggles and creaks,
A tangled ballet of laughter that peaks.
Together they dance, in a rhythm unseen,
Making music with silence, lively but keen.

Blossoming in the Moment

In a garden of giggles I unwind,
Where laughter sprouts, oh so kind.
Each chuckle a flower, bright and bold,
Stories of silliness waiting to be told.

Butterflies dance, no worries in sight,
They twirl and spin in pure delight.
A bee in a tux, sipping its tea,
As flowers wink at you and me.

The sun tickles leaves with a warm embrace,
A gnome on a swing, what a funny place!
We bloom with joy, take a break from the grind,
In this silly patch, peace is easy to find.

Oasis of Calm

In the desert of chaos, a mirage appears,
A pool full of laughter, washing away fears.
Floating on ducks with a quack and a splash,
Serenity bubbles when worries are dashed.

Cacti wear hats, what a whimsical scene,
A saguaro in shades, looking oh-so-keen.
The sun offers lemonade, ice cold and sweet,
While shadows bring chairs that dance to the beat.

Here, every cactus tells a joke or two,
In this funny oasis, I laugh with you.
The breeze carries giggles, like petals in flight,
Together we bloom in this laughable light.

The Stillness Between the Breaths

In the pause of a gasp, funny thoughts arise,
Like a rubber chicken, it squeaks and complies.
In stillness, I find giggles hidden away,
A tickle in silence, come out to play!

A zen master tripping, in search of his peace,
Stumbling on laughter, it never does cease.
Between inhaling and exhaling we find,
A world full of pranks, true joy intertwined.

Each breath is a joke, delivered just right,
I chuckle through whispers, holding on tight.
With the air filled with humor, worries go light,
In the space of the silence, everything's bright.

Serene Landscapes of the Mind

In the meadows of thought, where giggles abound,
Silly clouds float, never making a sound.
A tree wears a tutu, dancing just for fun,
Tickled by breezes, under the sun.

The stream babbles jokes, rippling with glee,
While fish flash their smiles, "Come laugh with me!"
Butterflies flutter with colorful flair,
They whisper sweet secrets, born from thin air.

Here in my mind, all the whimsical plays,
Create a bright canvas, a tapestry of rays.
Amongst flutters and chuckles, at peace we unwind,
In these calm landscapes, true joy we find.

The Gentle Art of Stillness

In the quiet of the day, we sit,
With coffee cups and not a single wit.
The squirrels debate with flair and pride,
While we simply ponder what we can't decide.

A snail slides by, taking its sweet time,
Laughing at us, lost in our own rhyme.
We stretch our legs, soon to nap away,
As nature giggles, 'Come out and play!'

A butterfly swirls, a tiny ballet,
As we chuckle at our plans gone astray.
Finding joy within, without a fuss,
Turns out, nature's just an old friend to trust.

So here we bask, lives slightly askew,
In the art of doing nothing, oh so true.
With laughter and peace hanging in the air,
In stillness, we find our blissful share.

Harmony in Nature's Canvas

The flowers dance with colors so bright,
While the ants march by, a comical sight.
Trees gossip softly, leaves whisper low,
With nature's giggles, putting on a show.

Bees buzz around with a humorous hum,
Ordering flowers, 'You're up next, come!'
A bird drops a twig—what a clumsy spree,
While we chuckle, savoring nature's glee.

The sun winks down, throwing golden rays,
Wrapping us in laughter, warming our days.
A frog leaps in, croaking one-liners, bold,
Nature's comedy show is never old.

So let us sketch this silly scene,
In the gallery of life, so vibrant and green.
With each splash of colors, laughter take flight,
In a world woven with humor, pure delight.

Flourishing in Silent Waters

The pond reflects a picture so still,
Where fish play tag with a thrilling skill.
A duck quacks jokes, floating by grand,
Making ripples of laughter across the land.

Turtles bask, wearing shells like hats,
With wisdom profound, they chat as chaps.
Each bubble that surfaces holds secrets of fun,
As they laugh at the ripples, each splash, each run.

Dragonflies zip like zany planes,
Chasing after the sun, ignoring the rains.
Nature's own circus, mischief on display,
We giggle together, brightening the day.

So let's raise a toast to water's deep grace,
To the chuckles that ripple, the joy we embrace.
In silent waters, laughter blooms free,
A state of pure fun, come sit with me.

Soft Echoes of Reflection

Mirrors of calm, where thoughts take flight,
As we ponder life, side by side, what a sight.
A frog croaks poetry from the nearby bog,
Echoes of laughter, nature's own dialogue.

Ripples tell tales of what's come and gone,
With the sun dipping low, twilight's yawn.
We hear the soft giggles of stars in the sky,
As crickets compose their songs, oh so spry.

Breezes whisper jokes only we can hear,
Carrying chuckles from far and near.
We sit in the quiet, reflecting our dreams,
Lost in the laughter of whispers and gleams.

So let's dance with shadows, weave tales anew,
Finding joy in reflections and what we do.
In echoes of laughter, together we dwell,
In a world of soft joy, all is well.

Lullabies of the Earth

In a garden, plants play peek-a-boo,
They giggle with the breeze, oh who knew!
With worms in top hats, dancing for fun,
While daisies wear shades, basking in sun.

The grass tickles toes as they prance,
While ladybugs tango in a tiny dance.
With crickets chirping their nightly tune,
And a moon that chuckles, a playful boon.

Bumblebees buzz like they're on a spree,
Spreading sweet whispers, oh so carefree.
The tulips all blush, a cheeky affair,
As butterflies flutter without a care.

So let's sing along to this joyful show,
In a world where laughter is sure to grow.
With every petal and giggle we find,
Joy blooms anew, leaving worries behind.

Soft Footprints in the Forest

In the forest, squirrels chatter with glee,
As they race each other, just wait and see!
With acorns as hats, they leap and bound,
While mushrooms nod softly, all around.

The trees wear their bark like a silly face,
And owls wink knowingly from their place.
While foxes tell jokes with their clever charm,
Beneath the bright stars, free from alarm.

A rabbit hops in, all dressed up neat,
With a carrot bouquet, isn't that sweet?
The flowers giggle, hiding behind leaves,
Sharing seedlings of laughter, as everyone believes.

So wander through here, let your spirit soar,
Join this woodland party and dance on the floor.
With twigs as your steps, let joy take its form,
In this playful haven, your heart will stay warm.

The Whispering Grove

In the grove, whispers of joy convene,
Where the wind plays tricks, always unseen.
The trees share secrets with giddy intent,
While bushes bend low, their laughter well spent.

A raccoon juggles shiny things he finds,
While owls hoot riddles, oh how it binds!
And the grasshoppers leap, wearing tiny crowns,
Making the squirrels giggle in their furry gowns.

The shadows dance lightly on the forest floor,
As sunlight peeks in, begging for more.
With giggles of petals, a fluttering cheer,
Every creature knows that fun is near.

So stroll through this grove, where laughter is rife,
A place where the mundane gets a new life.
With every soft whisper that tickles your ear,
You'll leave with a smile, and never a fear.

Beneath the Canopy of Serene Thoughts

Under the canopy of whimsical dreams,
Where the sunlight giggles and the moonlight beams.
A sloth hangs around, quite the lazy mate,
Cracking up jokes while he slowly gravitates.

The clouds above wear silly hats so bright,
As the rainbow giggles with pure delight.
While the brook babbles nonsense, a joyful stream,
Tickling the stones in a bubbly gleam.

Frogs croak a chorus that's truly absurd,
With turtles reciting each lovely word.
As butterflies flutter, dressed in their best,
Filling the air with a humor fest.

So lay here awhile, let your worries unfurl,
With the creatures who joke and the leaves that twirl.
In this whimsical glade, take a silly pause,
And savor the laughter in nature's applause.

The Silent Symphony of Growth

In the garden, whispers play,
A chipmunk waltzes every day,
The daisies can't stop giggling loud,
As ants march by, feeling quite proud.

The sunbeam tunes a golden tune,
While bumblebees hum like a cartoon,
In the soil, roots twist and twirl,
As nature hosts a leafy whirl.

A snail on stage takes a long bow,
The frogs echo 'Where's our big wow?'
Laughter blooms in shades so bright,
In this silent symphony, pure delight.

The Bud of Balanced Contentment

A sprout peeks from the earth's warm hug,
Pondering if it needs a shrug,
With such a weighty life ahead,
It asks the clouds if they're misled.

The wise old tree chuckles and sighs,
As the bud questions the vast blue skies,
'Just chill, my friend, take it slow,
Let time feed you, and you will grow.'

So here it sits, the bud aglow,
Plotting its path to the sun's show,
With a grin, it stretches its leaves,
Embracing the joy that truly weaves.

Threads of Tranquility

A spider spins a web with flair,
While squirrels play without a care,
The breeze provides a gentle tease,
As flowers sway like they're at a spree.

The daisies don their polka dots,
While butterflies plan daring plots,
A pebble jokes, 'I'm just a rock!'
In this garden, the laughter won't stop.

The wind chimes dance with delight,
On moonlit nights, they giggle bright,
So weaves a tapestry of cheer,
In nature's arms, we hold it dear.

Flourish Where Peace Blooms

The sunflowers tilt their heads in glee,
As bees buzz by, 'Is there honey for me?'
With every petal, joy unwinds,
In this place, happiness binds.

The grass tickles toes walking by,
While clouds play hide and seek in the sky,
Laughter echoes through the trees,
A symphony played in the summer breeze.

Leaves rustle softly, telling jokes,
As rabbits hop like friendly folks,
In the meadow of dreams, we find,
Happiness thrives, unconfined.

The Painted Canvas of Calm

In a world full of chatter, the colors collide,
A splash of mint green, where the giggles abide.
The trees paint a picture, oh what a delight,
With squirrels as artists, they dance in the light.

With umbrellas for bushes, a laughable sight,
A painted sky canvas, what a joyous flight!
The flowers wear hats, in a fashion parade,
Petals all fluttering, their bright colors played.

The sun tries to wink, as it's caught in a grin,
While clouds puff their cheeks, with a jolly spin.
Oh laughter erupts, from the ground to the sky,
In this painted calm, where the giggles fly.

So let's twirl in this garden, all carefree and wild,
With nature our canvas, happily styled.
Each brushstroke a moment, each leaf a good jest,
In this world of klutzes, we're certainly blessed.

Cultivating Mindful Meadows

In the meadow of laughter, where the daisies roam,
The bunnies are planning a funny little home.
With carrot-shaped pillows and a hopping spa,
They dance through the grass, saying, "Ha! Look at us—ha!"

The sun winks slyly, with a shine on its face,
As butterflies giggle, each in their own space.
They flutter and frolic, oh, what a parade,
While grasshoppers tap dance, in the sunshine's cascade.

With earthworms as DJ's, spinning tunes of delight,
The ants all groove gently, until the night.
The breeze joins the party, with a whoosh and a twirl,
While clovers are clapping, in a greenish whirl.

So cultivate chuckles, in this mindful scene,
Where nature's a circus, so vibrant and green.
With every small giggle, a smile will bloom,
In meadows of jests, let the joy surely loom.

Resting in Nature's Lap

Resting in green grass, all cozy and neat,
The ants are reporting, "This is quite the treat!"
A squirrel on a branch brings snacks for the crew,
With a nutty suggestion, "Let's have fun, just us two!"

The clouds float above, like fluffy sheep straying,
As the sun snaps a selfie, it's bright and displaying.
The daisies are gossiping, telling sly tales,
While a deer tries to swagger, but stumbles and fails.

With breezes that tickle, we giggle with glee,
While butterflies float like they're sipping sweet tea.
In nature's warm hug, all worries are lost,
Resting here feels lovely, no matter the cost.

So lay down your burdens, and hear nature's laughs,
As the creatures join in, creating funny crafts.
In this silly serenity, let your heart be light,
For resting with nature is pure delight.

Serenity Under the Canopy

Under the canopy's shade, where joy reigns supreme,
We'll have a grand picnic, with laughter as cream.
Ants in bowties, serving crumbs from a feast,
As a raccoon officiates, making fun of the least.

With birds in tuxedos, and frogs on a line,
The orchestra croaks as the sun starts to shine.
"Let's dance in the shadows!" chirps a sprightly lark,
While chipmunks in goggles build a rocket to spark.

The squirrels do the conga, in rhythm with trees,
While fireflies twinkle, like the stars in a breeze.
Laughter erupts, and the canopy sways,
In this world of hilarity, where joy stays ablaze.

So join in this chaos beneath leafy crowns,
Embrace the absurd in your finest of gowns.
For under this canopy, let your spirit run free,
In a riot of warmth, where we laugh with glee.

Beneath the Surface Calm

Beneath the waves, I float with glee,
A fish swims by, it's waving at me.
I hold my breath, a penguin's cheer,
The ocean's jokes whisper in my ear.

A seaweed tickle, what a delight,
A crab makes faces, oh what a sight!
With treasures found on the ocean floor,
Who knew such jokes could be found in score?

My snorkel's fogged, I can hardly see,
A dolphin laughs, 'come swim with me!'
Beneath this calm, the fun never ends,
In this watery world, you'll make new friends.

The Essence of Quietude

In the garden where the bunnies sun,
A turtle declares, 'I'm the fastest one!'
They hop and roll beneath the trees,
While I sip tea and enjoy the breeze.

The bees tell stories, buzzing with flair,
A sunflower yawns, 'Join me if you dare!'
They dance around, an airy ballet,
While I chuckle at how they play.

A ladybug winks, wearing her spots,
'Serious is boring,' she giggles a lot.
Chasing the butterflies, who wouldn't want,
To join in their laughter—a funny jaunt?

Cultivating Inner Bliss

With a trowel, I dig up fun,
A worm pops out, 'Let's all run!'
Planting daisies, I twist with delight,
A gnome nearby starts a pillow fight.

Sunshine smiles, it tickles my nose,
The flowers chuckle as the wind blows.
Patience is key, or so they say,
But I'd rather giggle the day away.

A squirrel steals seeds, that sneaky brat,
He stops to dance, and I join that chat.
Inner bliss, oh what a joke,
In this comedy of nature, who needs a cloak?

Petals of Peaceful Dreams

At twilight's glow, the moonlight beams,
I snuggle in soft petals, sweet dreams.
A pillow fight with wispy clouds,
Where laughter echoes, singing out loud.

The stars play tricks, they wink and tease,
While crickets chirp in silly keys.
'Oh dear,' I sigh, 'I can't sleep tight!'
As fireflies dance, I hold on tight.

Dreams swirl around, a merry mix,
With unicorns and giggling tricks.
This peaceful night, a comical scene,
Who knew dreams could be so serene?

A Breath of Gentle Blooms

In a garden where daisies dance,
Sunshine wears a polka-dot pants.
Bees buzz by, full of glee,
As if they've drank a cup of tea.

Worms wiggle in a silly parade,
Under the shade, they've all stayed.
Caterpillars munch with a grin,
Who knew snacks could be such a win?

Roses giggle, their thorns at rest,
Dandelions think they're the best.
A butterfly with a lazy swoop,
Declares, 'Join my happy troop!'

With petals soft as marshmallow fluff,
Life feels light, never too tough.
Each bloom a quirky little surprise,
In this garden where joy always lies.

The Embrace of Still Waters

A pond reflects a silly frog,
Settling in on a sunken log.
He croaks a tune so out of place,
Even the fish shake their face.

Ripples dance like a belly shake,
And ducks glide like they're on a break.
The lily pads play dress-up games,
While turtles take naps, deep in their frames.

A heron strikes a pose so grand,
While fish plot a splashy stand.
Crickets chat with utmost flair,
As dragonflies buzz without a care.

The stillness laughs, a chuckle soft,
As nature pretends to take off.
In waters calm, hilarity brews,
Embracing whimsy in every hue.

Traces of Calm in the Soil

Digging in dirt, oh what a sight,
Where worms wiggle with all their might.
Beetles strut, thinking they're kings,
While moles rumble, "Where's the bling?"

Roots stretch out like lazy cats,
Entwined in their bedtime chats.
Tunnels twist like a wiggly rhyme,
As earth giggles, lost in time.

Grasshoppers hop with bouncy cheer,
Amidst the soil, they have no fear.
Ants march with snacks, in a line,
"Join the parade—this food's divine!"

In the earth's embrace, laughter stirs,
With every squish, it's giggles and purrs.
Calm vibes swirl in burrows deep,
Where even the soil finds joy in sleep.

A Symphony of Leaves

Leaves rustle like a gossip crew,
Whispering secrets to me and you.
The oak cracks jokes, oh so wise,
While maples twirl in bright disguise.

With every breeze, they play a tune,
Dancing leaves, beneath the moon.
A chorus of laughter fills the air,
As squirrels shout, "You just can't compare!"

Each flutter sings a silly note,
While robins join in, oh what a quote!
"Life's a leaf, it's crazy fun,
So let's twirl till the day is done!"

Nature's symphony brings so much glee,
With each leaf's toss, we're wild and free.
In this playful grove, we find our cheer,
A melody of joy, loud and clear.

Tranquil Quotes from Nature

In the garden where giggles grow,
Earthworms ponder their next show.
A daisy winks, a rogue bee grins,
While butterflies share their silly sins.

The breeze whispers jokes, quite absurd,
While trees discuss how to dance like a nerd.
A squirrel spins tales, full of delight,
As clouds drift by, trying to take flight.

The sun beams down with a cheeky grin,
Tickling the flowers, coaxing them to spin.
Nature's laughter echoes, day in, day out,
Reminding us joy is what life's about.

So let us laugh, like the leaves in trees,
Join in the fun, wave your hands in the breeze.
Find humor in moments, big or small,
For in nature's joy, we can all stand tall.

A Petal's Soft Retreat

A petal rolled down on a lazy day,
Said, "Let's escape, let's run away!"
With a giggle it tumbled, oh what a sight,
Hoping for fortune, to spark some delight!

The flower beside it just sighed and said,
"You'll need more than whimsy to get ahead!"
But the petal just laughed, full of glee,
"I seek adventure, oh can't you see?"

With the wind as a chariot, off it went,
Dreams of outlandish places it lent.
Floating along, it danced with the breeze,
While dandelions chuckled, swaying with ease.

Oh, what a journey for one little leaf,
Giggling past butterflies, sharing belief.
In the end, it found joy, pure and sweet,
Life's more hilarious when you dance on your feet!

The Grounds of Mindful Existence

In the lush patch of laughter, the frogs croak,
Jokes about flies, as they happily poke.
"Why did the bug cross the path?" they jest,
"To join a hive-party, that's simply the best!"

A rabbit hops by, wearing a grin,
Says, "Life's an adventure, let the fun begin!"
He does a little jig, makes the daisies sway,
While ants march in line, planning their play.

Even the stones, all wise and serene,
Share puns about paths and where they have been.
"Rock and roll," they chuckle, "it's essential,
To find joy in stillness, it's quite fundamental!"

So let's gather round in this circus of greens,
With laughter galore as light-hearted queens.
Mindful existence is a chuckle-filled ride,
Join nature's fun, let joy be your guide!

Resting on a Cushion of Calm

On a fluffy cloud, the kittens do play,
Chasing rainbows, in their own quilted way.
With each little leap, they giggle and twirl,
Purring soft secrets, giving joy a whirl.

The sun beams down, a warm, fuzzy hug,
While a lazy caterpillar gives a gentle shrug.
"Life's a vast garden, filled with sweet dreams,
Just relax, my friend, nothing's as it seems."

A pair of wise owls, hooting with glee,
Share jokes about shadows and flying free.
"One day we'll soar, without a care,
But for now, let's snooze, life's a cozy affair!"

So rest your spirit on this feather-bright bed,
Savor each moment, let laughter be spread.
For in this cushion of calm, we'll find,
The smoothness of giggles, our hearts intertwined.

Embrace of Gentle Roots

In the soil, the worms do dance,
A wiggle here, a little prance.
They don't care 'bout their look or size,
Just diggin' deep beneath the skies.

Sunshine laughs in golden rays,
While daisies break into a daze.
Who knew that petals wore such flair?
They're the fashionistas of the air!

Bees humming tunes, quite the band,
Buzzing round the flowers, oh so grand.
"Oh daffodil, you stole my heart!"
"Don't worry, lily, we won't part!"

A garden where giggles grow,
Worms and blooms just put on a show.
Nature's jesters in a leafy play,
Inviting chuckles every day.

The Calm Within the Garden

In the beds where veggies lay,
Tomatoes peek and shout, "Hooray!"
Carrots grinning underground,
While lettuce fluffs, round and proud.

The radishes hold a secret club,
"What's the gossip?" "Oh, just shrubs!"
They sip their dew from leaves so sweet,
While busy ants march to the beat.

Chickens cluck with a flair for rhyme,
"Eggs are art, and it's breakfast time!"
While turkeys strut with proud delight,
Dreaming of Thanksgiving, what a sight!

A scarecrow tall with a floppy hat,
Whispers jokes to the little brat:
"Why did the seed take a nap?"
"Because it was a little sap!"

Hushed Echoes of Nature

Crickets chirp in playful rhyme,
Playing catch with the passing time.
A frog leaps up to join the fun,
"Ribbit! Ribbit! Where's everyone?"

Butterflies float with a fluttering cheer,
Catching whispers of the atmosphere.
"Did you hear what the flower said?"
"Shh, keep it down, I'm trying to spread!"

Clouds roll by like sheep on parade,
Dreamy thoughts in the sunlight cascade.
While the wind plays tag with a leaf,
"Oh dear leaf, don't be so brief!"

A snail slips past with a gooey smile,
"Slow and steady wins the style!"
Nature giggles in its vibrant spree,
Who knew serenity could be so silly?

Tranquility in Bloom

Buds pop open like a soda can,
"Chill out, beans, don't be a fan!"
Ivy slips in a sportsy line,
"Growing's easy; just sip some brine!"

The sunbeam tickles the daisies bright,
"Sorry, late! I lost my light!"
And in the breeze the leaves do sway,
"Let's dance, folks, it's a leafy day!"

Mice play tag 'round the sunflower grin,
"Who's it? Not me, let the games begin!"
With a wink, they dart through the patch,
"Catch me if you can, good luck with that!"

In every nook, joy takes a bloom,
A snapshot of laughter hangs in the room.
So here's to nature's quirky delight,
In her quietness, there's so much light!

Soft Currents of Stillness

In a pond so calm and wide,
Frogs croak jokes with great delight.
Fish swim by with silly grins,
And turtles giggle at their fins.

Grasshoppers bounce on lazy grass,
Chasing dreams that come to pass.
Each rustle brings a chuckle light,
As squirrels plot their comic flight.

The breeze whispers tales of cheer,
While crickets hum – 'What are we here?'
Underneath the willow's sway,
The world's just one big cabaret!

So let the laughter fill the air,
As nature's jokes, beyond compare.
With every quirk that earth bestows,
We find the smiles in life's cute prose.

The Quiet of Morning Dew

Morning breaks with drops so small,
Like beads of joy that lightly fall.
A spider spins a web of dreams,
While ants form lines and plot their schemes.

Worms poke heads out, sport a grin,
While coiled snakes play hide and spin.
The world awakes, with laughs anew,
In early glow where dew shines through.

Birds gossip in chirpy tones,
About the biggest worms and bones.
As sunbeams tickle sleepy leaves,
Nature laughs, and so she breathes.

So join the dance of playful hues,
Where laughter flows like morning dew.
In every drop, a joke is spun,
The day begins – let's have some fun!

Blossoms Beneath a Starlit Sky

Under stars that twinkle bright,
Flowers tell of their midnight flight.
Petals giggle, swaying low,
While moonbeams join the flower show.

Bees buzz softly, spinning tales,
Of honey joys and slimy snails.
In the night, the crickets play,
Creating tunes in the ballet.

A breeze tickles the sleeping buds,
And fireflies leap like little thuds.
Together they dance, a glowing crew,
Painting the air with laughs anew.

So 'neath the stars where mischief gleams,
Nature whispers all her dreams.
With every bloom and twinkling eye,
Life's just a jest, oh my, oh my!

Nature's Gentle Embrace

A cozy nook where flowers bloom,
Squirrels chatter, making room.
The sun shines down, a golden ray,
While shadows play in a funny way.

Butterflies in polka dots,
Flit around like silly shots.
Nature says, 'Forget your worries,'
As daisies spin in gentle flurries.

The wind whistles tunes of glee,
Inviting all to dance and see.
In every breath, a joke is cast,
With laughter echoing, unsurpassed.

So take a step and join the cheer,
In nature's arms, there's naught to fear.
Let joy be found in every space,
In life's warm and gentle embrace.

Quietude Among the Leaves

Whispers dance upon the breeze,
A squirrel plotting with such ease.
Leaves giggle at a passing bee,
While ants conspire near a tree.

Branches sway, they play a tune,
A caterpillar prances, oh so strewn!
While the grass softly chortles below,
A perfect stage for nature's show.

Quiet moments, so absurd,
A flower jokes, it's quite unheard.
The sun grins down, a craft so neat,
As laughter echoes with the heat.

Life's a riot in shades of green,
Where every leaf's a jester seen.
Among the quietude they throng,
In a world where humor sings along.

Blossoms Beneath the Moonlight

Petals sway in silver light,
A gopher woos a moth tonight.
Moonbeams tickle dew-kissed blooms,
While crickets strut with witty tunes.

Underneath this starry dome,
A flower declares it's far from home.
'Why so glum?' a moonbeam mocks,
'At least you're not just hiding rocks!'

A silly breeze begins to laugh,
As shadows pirouette on the path.
Blooms exchange their chirpy tales,
Of rivalries in wind-fueled gales.

So in this garden fair and bright,
Laughter blooms with pure delight.
Underneath the moon's warm grin,
The night is where the fun begins.

The Unseen Garden of Peace

In a patch where no one goes,
A dandelion steals the show,
With roots that wiggle and a big grin,
It tickles the soil, welcoming kin.

A hedgehog hides with quite the flair,
His prickles raise a curious hair.
'Wanna join my hibernation spree?'
He chirps, 'And let's forget the tea!'

The flowers plot a Sunday dance,
While weeds pull pranks, a leafy chance.
'Why must you stretch so tall?' they plead,
'This garden's ours!' says a cheeky seed.

Peace is odd in places obscure,
As giggles spread, the roots endure.
In this unseen wonderland of cheer,
Life's a party, full of queer.

Calm Reflections in a Still Pond

Ripples giggle at a frog's big leap,
While lily pads hold secrets deep.
A fish debates with a dragonfly,
'Who's faster?' they laugh as time glides by.

The sky woos the water in a glance,
Sunsets paint a golden dance.
Amid the calm, a heron strikes a pose,
While a turtle chuckles at his toes.

A splash of humor hides in the gloom,
As pond life blooms in quiet room.
'Tell me, friends, what's the best joke?'
As reeds sway gently—nature's cloak.

In stillness, laughter travels wide,
Where peace and whimsy now abide.
Reflections dance beneath the glow,
In this serene pond, fun grows slow.

The Tenderness of Solitude

In a chair with a view, I make my retreat,
Where socks on the floor form a cozy seat.
The cat steals my sandwich, gives me a wink,
As I ponder the deep thoughts of peanut butter and pink.

Dreams float like fluff on a warm summer breeze,
While I dodge the dishes with the greatest of ease.
My time, oh so precious, like goldfish on ice,
I chuckle at life's little quirks and precise.

What joy in the silence, it grumbles and sighs,
With a laundry basket laughing, oh how time flies!
The clock ticks loudly, in turbulent glee,
As I revel in moments of just being me.

So here in this chaos, I'll plant my own bliss,
In a garden of laughter, not a thing I would miss.
When solitude beckons, I'm all ears and cheer,
Life's absurdities keep me smiling, my dear.

Haven of Hopeful Flora

In this garden of giggles, blooms with delight,
Where daisies wear sunglasses, oh what a sight!
The roses hum tunes, serenading the bees,
While daisies play chess with the wise old trees.

A tomato in sneakers races by in a blur,
Chasing a carrot who just heard a purr.
In this haven of laughter, oh how plants play,
With worms as the referees, it's a grand day!

Each petal a chuckle, each stem a new jest,
The tulips are gossiping, thinking they're best.
In this funny little corner, joy blooms so bright,
As I sip lemonade, under the sun's light.

Who knew shrubbery could throw such a bash?
With laughter and growth, it's a floral splash!
In my haven where pie and daffodils sing,
I'm planting my dreams on the backs of spring.

Ripples of Rapture

A pond with reflections that dance with delight,
Where frogs wear top hats in the soft evening light.
They leap to the rhythm of a cricket's grand tune,
Creating a splash, like July in June.

The fish trade their whispers, in bubbles they share,
As water lilies giggle without any care.
A duck in a bowtie glides by, oh so sly,
While dragonflies plot, as they swish and they fly.

With each gentle ripple, the world gets a shake,
A turtle on stilts dreams of making a cake.
Ripples of rapture spill joy on the leaves,
As the sunlight glimmers, and the humor weaves.

In this comedy realm where the wild things play,
I snorkel in laughter, come join in the fray!
For every splash echoes, like giggles in air,
In the magic of moments that spark flair.

Nectar of Nonchalance

In a hive where the bees take the day off to play,
They sip on the nectar, in a carefree way.
With flowers all around, they dance with such glee,
These charming young pollinators just buzzing with spree.

A butterfly flutters, adorned in bright hues,
Telling tales of a sunbeam and sipping on dew.
With petals like jokes, all like puns in disguise,
In the warmth of this garden, humor never dies.

The ants throw a party, in a crumb-laden feast,
Where laughter and crumbs abound, never the least.
As they waltz with a wink, and strut in a line,
Their tiny parade, oh, it can't help but shine!

Here's nectar of nonsense, in each buzzing sound,
Where silliness blooms, growing freely around.
So come take a moment, just linger and sway,
In the buzz of the day where silliness stays.

Flourishing in Stillness

In the garden of my mind, I sit,
Weeds of worry, I choose to admit.
A dandelion dreams with a silly grin,
Tickling the daisies, let the fun begin.

The sun's warm laughter spills on my toes,
It's a playful dance, as the breeze gently blows.
While butterflies giggle in their bright spree,
I ponder if crickets can also be free.

With a cup of tea and a hat that's too wide,
I sip my thoughts on a bouncy slide.
Each sip a chuckle, each drop a cheer,
Finding joy in the calm, it's becoming clear.

So let's giggle with grass and titter with trees,
Chasing calm like a runaway breeze.
For in life's stillness, I see the jest,
Laughing through moments, I feel truly blessed.

Tending to the Inner Grove

In the woods of my heart, there's a ruckus and cheer,
A squirrel named Peanut is hiding my beer.
While leaves gossip softly, they chuckle quite loud,
And the mushrooms make jokes, oh, they're terribly proud.

I tend to my grove with a trowel and grin,
Unruly branches and rogue roots begin.
Poking the soil, I wiggle my toes,
Who knew that nature could tickle like prose?

The owls hoot in rhymes, wisecracking delight,
While rabbits sport ties, dressed for a fight.
I'm pruning my thoughts, snipping with flair,
Each snip brings a giggle, floating in air.

So here's to the gnomes with their glittery jest,
Who find every moment a laughable quest.
Tending to laughter, I nurture my bliss,
In the grove of my being, serenity's kiss.

The Balm of Nature's Breath

Inhale the giggles of the leafy trees,
Exhaling chuckles carried by the breeze.
Every breath a bubble, bursting with fun,
Nature's a comedian, under the sun.

Dandelion tickles on my nose make me sneeze,
While the grass whispers secrets with mischievous ease.
Mushrooms are the wise guys, clever and spry,
With caps like hats, oh, the jokes they could try!

The brook's bubbling laughter, a playful song,
Sings stories of wanderers who've wandered along.
Each pebble a punchline, each ripple a mime,
Nature's a stand-up, and it's always prime time.

So let's take a stroll where the funny folks play,
Where whimsy and warmth hold dull thoughts at bay.
In the balm of fresh air, I treasure my mirth,
Finding joy in the twists of this wild world's girth.

Tranquil Pathways

Strolling on paths where the daisies chat,
Fluffy clouds gossip, wearing the sun like a hat.
The trees wear their smiles, oh so bright,
As squirrels do karate, what an odd sight!

On this tranquil journey, I stumble and giggle,
A tumble of laughter, my thoughts softly wiggle.
Crickets crack jokes, while pebbles jump in glee,
It's a riot of joy, just nature and me.

The wind has a tickle that dances through hair,
As if each soft whisper is teasing a dare.
With a butterfly brigade leading the way,
I'm swept in the silliness, come what may.

So let's walk together, with chuckles unbound,
On pathways of warmth that wrap all around.
In the quietest corners where fun has its reign,
I find my heart blooming like flowered terrain.

Meadow of Mellow Moments

In fields where daisies twist and twirl,
Laughter blooms with every swirl.
Butterflies dance, the sun's a tease,
Even ants parade with utmost ease.

The grass whispers secrets, oh so sly,
As rabbits hop and pretend to fly.
Clouds play tag, a fluffy brigade,
In this meadow, all worries fade.

Chickens cluck jokes, a real crowing show,
While squirrels giggle as they go.
Every inch, a joke to behold,
With punchlines sprouting like marigold.

So let us laugh and lose our cares,
In this meadow where giggles flare.
With joy as bright as a sunflower's hue,
Here's a wink and a chuckle, just for you!

The Language of Quietude

In stillness wrapped, a hush surrounds,
Where even shadows make soft sounds.
Whispers of wind play hide and seek,
With giggles of leaves, the trees all speak.

The brook joins in, a bubbly delight,
Tickling rocks with laughter, what a sight!
Each ripple a chuckle, so sweet and bright,
Nature's own stand-up, day and night.

A snail slides by with a funny grace,
Wearing a shell like a slow car pace.
It winks at a frog, who's cracking a grin,
In silence, the humor begins to spin.

A warm sunbeam nudges the lazy cat,
Who yawns, then stretches, all plump and fat.
In this language quiet, funny and sly,
Laughter whispers softly, as time floats by.

Serenity's Hidden Oasis

In a corner of calm, there's laughter afloat,
Where the cactus wears shades on its little coat.
Palms sway in rhythm, a tropical tune,
As the sun hands out smiles, quite opportune.

Misfit geese sporting a festive parade,
Flap-flop through waters, their troubles delayed.
A turtle tells tales with a slow, sly wink,
While fish gather 'round for gossip and drink.

The lemonade fountain bursts bubbles galore,
While flamingos gossip, what fun they implore.
Sunset spills hues, a painter's embrace,
In this oasis, it's a playful race.

Amidst the calm, the mirth takes flight,
As each furry creature joins in the light.
In this world where laughter is simply pure,
An oasis of giggles, the heart feels secure.

Harmony in the Heart of the Woods

In the woods where the tall trees sway,
A raccoon plays tunes in a merry ballet.
Squirrels hold concerts, a nutty delight,
With acorns aplenty, they dance through the night.

Frogs in the bogs all croak a tune,
Competing for fame, like pop stars in June.
Fireflies twinkle, they light up the show,
Twirling with giggles, they steal the flow.

An old owl chuckles, wise and refined,
"Whoo" is the punchline, so cleverly defined.
Mice are the backup, all dressed in style,
Squeaking in harmony, they stretch a long mile.

Amidst the chaos, a calm takes its turn,
As laughter and nature together do churn.
In the heart of the woods, where fun never fades,
The spirit of joy in every glade.

The Tranquil Tapestry

In a garden of socks, bright and loud,
Tangled weeds dance in a shroud.
The daisies giggle, a ticklish spree,
Sunflowers don hats; what a sight to see!

Ants have meetings, plotting their quests,
Over crumbs from picnics, they're true guests.
Bees buzz in suits, sipping sweet tea,
A pie on the windowsill, come join the jamboree!

Amidst the chaos, a frog strikes a pose,
Sips on his latte, in sunlight, he doze.
A cat serenades, with a dramatic flair,
While rabbits hop by, all without a care.

Leaves rustle softly and whisper a joke,
The trees share laughter, in this wild yoke.
In this realm of joy, every frown flips,
Life's a whimsical ride, embrace the trips!

Between Shadows and Light

A chameleon sits, pondering the hue,
Wondering if blue suits him too.
A shadow plays tag with a flickering glow,
While squirrels toss acorns; oh, what a show!

The sun rolls around like a jolly old man,
Chasing clouds in a comedic plan.
Grasshoppers leap in a jazz-riffed delight,
Syncopated rhythms, under the moonlight.

A duck in a bowtie leads the parade,
With feathery friends, they've come out unafraid.
In puddles they prance, splashing with glee,
Painting reflections, creating a spree!

The night whispers secrets, while twinkles lay low,
The breeze carries chuckles, a gentle flow.
Between shadows and light, the laughter unites,
In this grand escapade, all worries take flight!

Gentle Currents of Contentment

A river sings softly, a bubbling prank,
With fish doing backstrokes, oh, how they flank.
A turtle in glasses reads the fine print,
While otters play chess, they never hint.

Cattails sway like they're in the groove,
As frogs hold auditions, trying to prove.
The sky paints cartoons with whimsical flair,
While clouds roll by, plotting lighthearted dare!

Fireflies twinkle, throwing a rave,
Dancing in circles, feeling quite brave.
The moon writes poetry, in silver ink,
While crickets recite, with wit on the brink.

All drift together, in this bright ballet,
Nothing but chuckles guiding the way.
In gentle waters, where laughter flows free,
Every splash is a giggle; come join the spree!

Rooms of Reverie

In rooms filled with color, laughter abounds,
Where ticklish paintbrushes make giggly sounds.
A couch of marshmallows, plump and round,
Here, candy canes dance, joyfully unbound.

A chandelier of jellies swings to and fro,
While cake batter curtains flutter in tow.
Each corner is filled with silly delight,
As cupcakes play chess, in the soft candlelight.

Posters of silly faces adorn every wall,
And a raccoon DJ spins tracks at the hall.
The floor is a trampoline, bouncy and sweet,
Where socks turn into superheroes; can't take a seat!

In rooms of reverie, dreams take a stand,
Life is a party, oh, isn't it grand?
With laughter echoing, bright as the sun,
In this whimsical realm, we all come as one!

Tides of Restfulness

Waves of laughter roll in tight,
As we chase the moon at night.
Tides that tickle toes and feet,
Bring the joy that feels so sweet.

Sailing boats made of our dreams,
Float on lazy, sunlit beams.
Paddling through the giggles' sound,
We play hide and seek with found.

Fluffy clouds like cotton candy,
Drift in skies that feel quite handy.
Splashing colors, bright and bold,
Tell a story yet untold.

So let the breezes spin around,
Whispers of fun, there's joy abound.
Find your peace in laughter's grace,
Let your worries keep their pace.

Serenity in the Silence

Whispers wander in the shade,
Where even squirrels are delayed.
Breezes chuckle, leaves go 'whoosh',
As nature's joke makes us all swoosh.

Crunchy snacks from forest treats,
Every crumb is life's sweet feats.
Stillness giggles in the air,
While frogs discuss their latest dare.

Birds are chirping with delight,
Telling tales of morning's flight.
The world hums a zany tune,
Even flowers dance at noon.

So sit back, enjoy the play,
Nature's antics make our day.
In the stillness, find your cheer,
As joy and silence quite adhere.

Echoing Calm After the Storm

Thunder booms like laughter loud,
Clouds parade a shimm'ring shroud.
"Did we dance too hard?" they say,
While puddles splash in bright array.

Raindrops tickle windowpanes,
Singing songs of gentle rains.
Lightning's joke has passed us by,
Now sunshine's grin spreads in the sky.

Nature yawns, shakes off the dread,
As moonlight dances on our bed.
Calm erupts like fizzy soda,
Twirling joy that's in the quota.

So here's to calm after the fight,
Where giggles bloom and dreams take flight.
Let's share a laugh, enjoy the breeze,
In cozy moments, find the ease.

Nurtured by the Earth

Beneath the soil, lots of fun,
Worms wiggle, basking in the sun.
Roots are giggling all around,
While daisies dance upon the ground.

Ants form a line, a silly parade,
Crafting paths that nature made.
In the garden, jokes are spread,
Even vegetables laugh in red.

Flowers tease with colors bright,
Whispering secrets through the night.
Bees buzz tunes of honeyed cheer,
A symphony for all to hear.

So lose yourself in earth's delight,
Let nature's humor take its flight.
In every bud, a jest you'll find,
Laughter thrives, we're all aligned.

Roots of Peace

In a quiet garden, a gnome takes a nap,
With dreams of a world that's free from the crap.
The daisies are dancing, they're light on their toes,
While the broccoli claims that it knows how to pose.

The carrots all chuckle, they tickle the leaves,
Saying peace is found under the tree, if you please!
A potato rolls over, a brave little spud,
Yelling, 'In this patch, we've got chaos to shun!'

The cabbages whisper, conspiracy chat,
About how to outsmart that old rascally cat.
A root's got a plan, it's peculiar but bright,
To lead all the veggies to a peaceful night.

So while nature's up to its humorous tricks,
Remember that laughter is the best kind of fix.
The roots deep in soil, they know what to seek,
In the laughter of greens, assurance is chic.

Blossoms of Stillness

Beneath the tall roses, a snail makes his bed,
With a pillow of petals, all gentle, no dread.
The violets giggle as they sway with the breeze,
While the tulips shout, 'We're just here to tease!'

A butterfly flutters, he thinks he's so grand,
But the daisies just roll their eyes at his plan.
They whisper of stories, of times long ago,
When they caused quite a ruckus with their sunflower show.

The peonies yawn, they've no cares in the world,
While the wind carries gossip, a secret unfurled,
Of a bee who got stuck in a caramel mess,
Now buzzing with laughter, he's feeling quite blessed.

So amidst the stillness, there's humor afloat,
As blossoms remind us to cherish and gloat.
A giggle in petals is all that we need,
In the realm of the garden, joy's always the creed.

Harmony in the Hush

In the hush of the night, an owl strikes a pose,
While the crickets compose their own little prose.
Silence holds hands with the sly summer breeze,
As they giggle together, spreading joy with ease.

The moon winks at shadows that dance on the ground,
While the fireflies twinkle, a light show profound.
A toad croaks a joke, to the stars up above,
And the chorus of night sings out with love.

The bushes all chuckle, they're thick with surprise,
At the antics of critters and their clever lies.
In the still of the woods, where the laughter is light,
Harmonic the whispers, all golden and bright.

So when darkness enfolds, and the world seems asleep,
Remember the joy, the secrets we keep.
In harmony hush, with a wink and a grin,
The world softly chuckles, let the good times begin!

Serenity in Subtle Growth

Once upon a sprout, a worm shared his thoughts,
On how quiet growth brings the best kind of plots.
He spoke with a wisdom that made others grin,
While sharing his secrets, they chuckled within.

A little green herb claimed it knew all the tricks,
To grow in the shade while avoiding the pricks.
The lettuce around him just nodded in glee,
As they plotted their plans for tea parties, you see.

A sunflower mutters about sunbeams so bright,
While the radishes joke about taking a flight.
They laugh and they giggle, so merry and spry,
While stretching their leaves to reach up to the sky.

In the realm of the garden, together they thrive,
With mischief and joy, they most surely arrive.
For growth may be subtle, but laughter is loud;
With a wink and a giggle, they stand all so proud.

www.ingramcontent.com/pod-product-compliance
Lightning Source LLC
Chambersburg PA
CBHW071844160426
43209CB00003B/411